PIANO · VOCAL · GUITAR

The Big Book of Big Band Hits

The BIG BOOK OF BIG BAND Hits

ISBN 0-634-02246-6

HAL • LEONARD®
CORPORATION

7777 W. BLUEMOUND RD. P.O. BOX 13819 MILWAUKEE, WI 53213

Visit Hal Leonard Online at
www.halleonard.com

Contents

AIR MAIL SPECIAL

By BENNY GOODMAN, JIMMY MUNDY
and CHARLIE CHRISTIAN

ALRIGHT, OKAY, YOU WIN

Words and Music by SID WYCHE
and MAYME WATTS

Moderately, with rhythm

AMOR
(Amor, Amor, Amor)

Music by GABRIEL RUIZ
Spanish Words by RICARDO LOPEZ MENDEZ
English Words by NORMAN NEWELL

BÉSAME MUCHO
(Kiss Me Much)

Music and Spanish Words by
CONSUELO VELAZQUEZ
English Words by SUNNY SKYLAR

THE BEST THINGS HAPPEN WHILE YOU'RE DANCING

from the Motion Picture Irving Berlin's WHITE CHRISTMAS

Words and Music by
IRVING BERLIN

Lyrics:

The best things _____ hap-pen while you're danc-ing. _____ Things that you would not do at home come nat-ur-'lly on the floor. _____ For

BLUE CHAMPAGNE

Words and Music by GRADY WATTS,
FRANK RYERSON and JIMMY EATON

Slowly

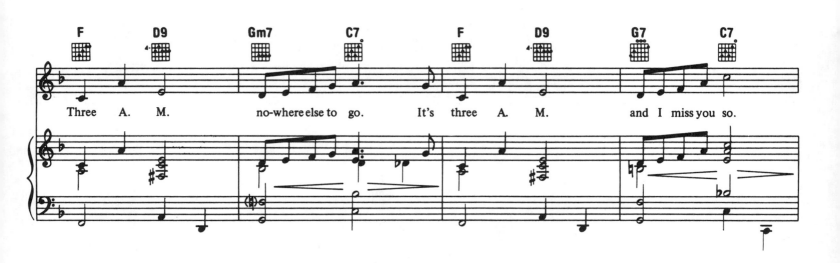

Three A. M. no-where else to go. It's three A. M. and I miss you so.

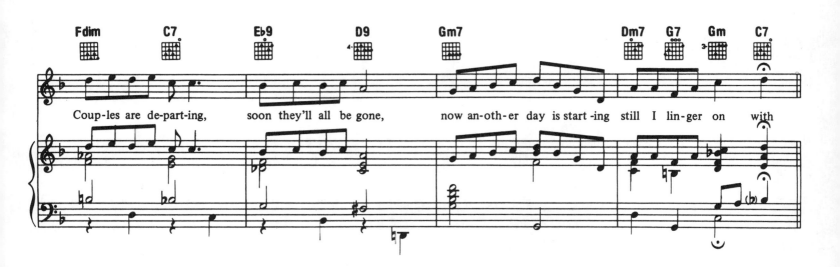

Coup-les are de-part-ing, soon they'll all be gone, now an-oth-er day is start-ing still I lin-ger on with

BODY AND SOUL

Words by EDWARD HEYMAN,
ROBERT SOUR and FRANK EYTON
Music by JOHN GREEN

dance to prove, dear. My life a wreck you're mak - ing,

you know I'm yours for just the tak - ing; I'd glad - ly sur -

ren - der my - self to you, bod - y and

soul!

soul!

CARAVAN

Words and Music by DUKE ELLINGTON,
IRVING MILLS and JUAN TIZOL

CALDONIA
(What Makes Your Big Head So Hard?)

Words and Music by
FLEECIE MOORE

Medium boogie woogie tempo

don-ia! ___ Cal-don-ia! ___ What Makes Your Big Head So Hard?

CAN'T GET OUT OF THIS MOOD

Words and Music by FRANK LOESSER
and JIMMY McHUGH

CHEROKEE
(Indian Love Song)

Words and Music by
RAY NOBLE

FLAT FOOT FLOOGIE

Words and Music by SLIM GAILLARD,
SLAM STEWART and BUD GREEN

Moderato (*with swing*)

Voice

There's a new kill-er dil-ler There's a new har-lem thrill-er

A new way to ru-in the rugs A new dance for "Jit-ter Bugs."

Chorus

THE FLAT FOOT FLOOGEE with the Floy Floy THE FLAT FOOT FLOOGEE with the

48

* Pronounced so as to rhyme with "HOW"

CHRISTOPHER COLUMBUS

Lyric by ANDY RAZAF
Music by LEON BERRY

CIRIBIRIBIN

Based on the original melody
by A. PESTALOZZA
English Version by HARRY JAMES
and JACK LAWRENCE

DON'T GET AROUND MUCH ANYMORE

Words and Music by DUKE ELLINGTON
and BOB RUSSELL

EVERYTHING HAPPENS TO ME

Words by TOM ADAIR
Music by MATT DENNIS

Slowly
p-f
Cm9 F9 Dm7 B♭dim Cm7 F7+5
make a date for golf and you can bet your life it rains, I try to give a part-y and the
Dm7-5 G7 Bdim E♭m6 Dm7 G7sus G7
guy up-stairs com-plains, I guess I'll go thru life just catch-in' colds and miss-in' trains.
Cm7 B7 B♭ Cm9 F9
Ev-'ry-thing hap-pens to me. I nev-er miss a thing, I've had the
Dm7 B♭dim Cm7 F7+5 Dm7-5 G7
meas-les and the mumps, and ev-'ry time I play an ace my part-ner al-ways trumps, I

FLYING HOME

Music by BENNY GOODMAN
and LIONEL HAMPTON
Lyric by SID ROBIN

HIT THE ROAD TO DREAMLAND
from the Paramount Picture STAR SPANGLED RHYTHM

Words by JOHNNY MERCER
Music by HAROLD ARLEN

HEART AND SOUL
from the Paramount Short Subject A SONG IS BORN

Words by FRANK LOESSER
Music by HOAGY CARMICHAEL

Moderately, lightly rhythmical

Heart and soul, _____ I fell in love with you. Heart and soul, _____

_____ the way a fool would do, mad - ly, _____ be - cause you held me

tight and stole a kiss in the night. Heart and soul, _____

_____ I begged to be a - dored. Lost con - trol _____ and tum - bled o - ver - board

HELLO, MY LOVER, GOODBYE

Words by EDWARD HEYMAN
Music by JOHNNY GREEN

Love is a leg-end grown dim-mer and dim-mer. There's noth-ing left ___ but the

ti-ni-est glim-mer of hope. ___

Where is the one ___ who will make my life sun-lit? Where is the kiss ___ that will

HOORAY FOR LOVE

Lyric by LEO ROBIN
Music by HAROLD ARLEN

I CAN'T GET STARTED WITH YOU

Words by IRA GERSHWIN
Music by VERNON DUKE

I CAN DREAM, CAN'T I?

Lyric by IRVING KAHAL
Music by SAMMY FAIN

I DIDN'T KNOW WHAT TIME IT WAS

Words by LORENZ HART
Music by RICHARD RODGERS

I HEAR MUSIC

from the Paramount Picture DANCING ON A DIME

Words by FRANK LOESSER
Music by BURTON LANE

I'LL GET BY
(As Long as I Have You)

Lyric by ROY TURK
Music by FRED E. AHLERT

I LET A SONG GO OUT OF MY HEART

Words and Music by DUKE ELLINGTON,
HENRY NEMO, JOHN REDMOND and IRVING MILLS

I'LL BE SEEING YOU

Lyric by IRVING KAHAL
Music by SAMMY FAIN

Ca-the-dral bells were toll - ing ____ And our hearts sang on, ___ Was it the spell of Par - is ____ Or the A - pril dawn? ____ Who knows, ____ if we shall meet a - gain? ____

I'VE GOT MY LOVE TO KEEP ME WARM

from the 20th Century Fox Motion Picture ON THE AVENUE

Words and Music by
IRVING BERLIN

Lyrics:

The snow is snow-ing, the wind is blow-ing, but I can weath-er the storm.

What do I care how much it may storm?

I'VE HEARD THAT SONG BEFORE

Lyric by SAMMY CAHN
Music by JULE STYNE

IF YOU CAN'T SING IT
(You'll Have to Swing It)

from the Paramount Picture RHYTHM ON THE RANGE

Words and Music by
SAM COSLOW

121

IT'S EASY TO REMEMBER

from the Paramount Picture MISSISSIPPI

Words by LORENZ HART
Music by RICHARD RODGERS

IN THE MOOD

By JOE GARLAND

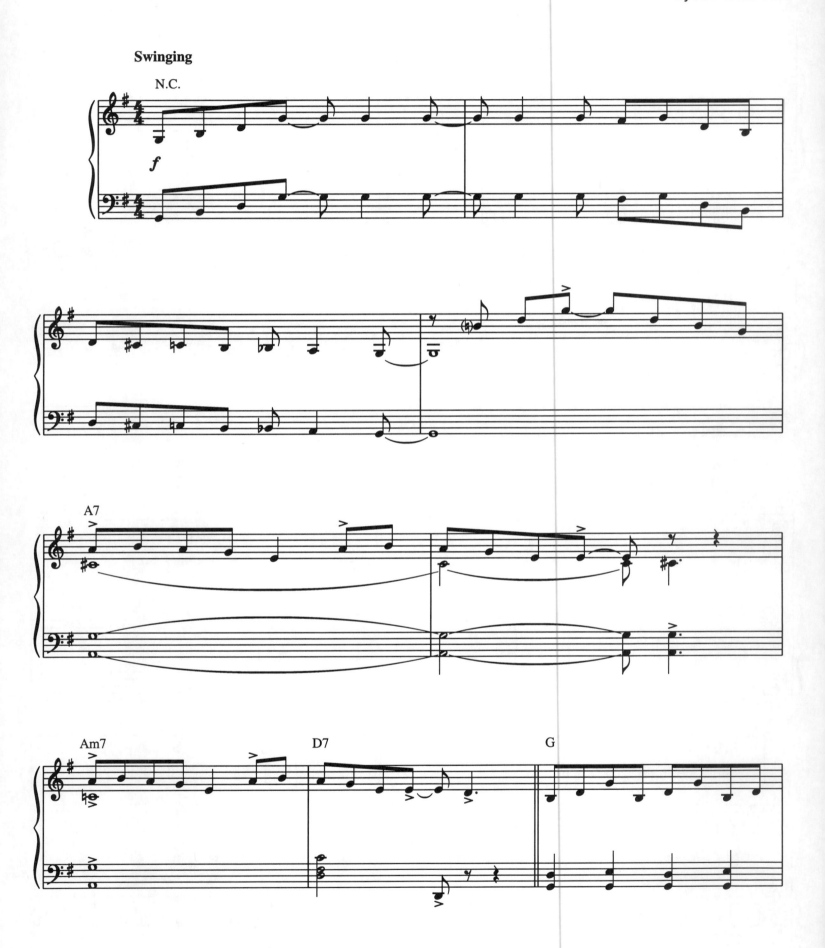

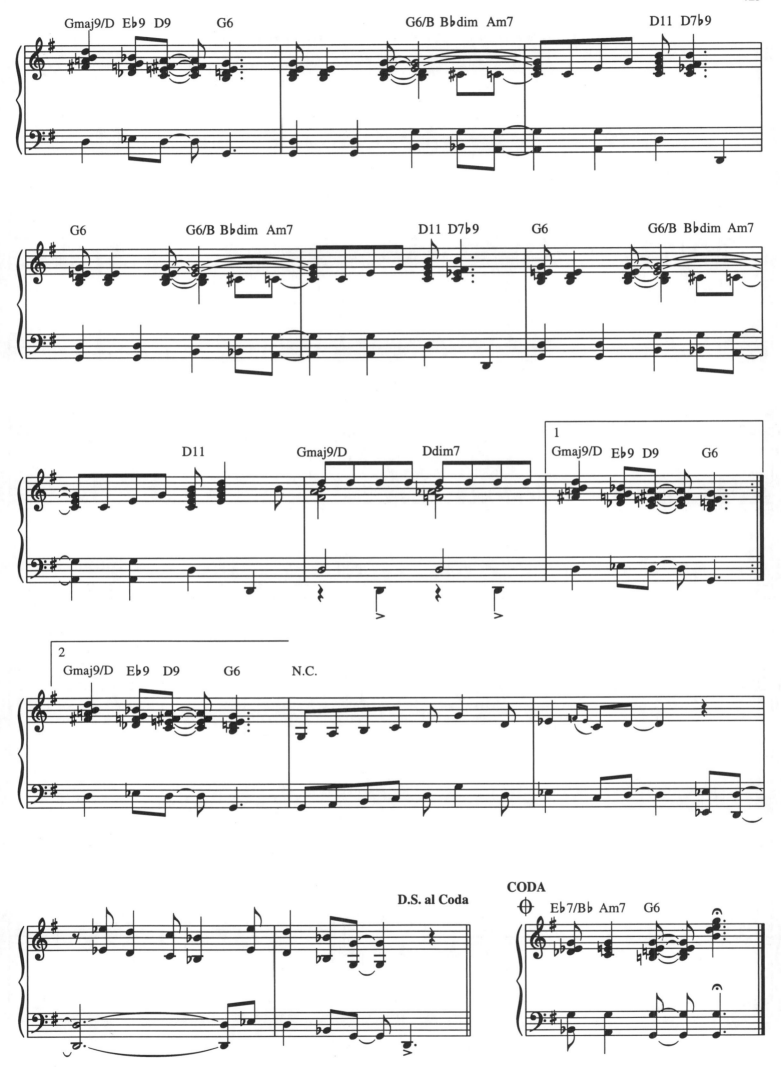

IT COULD HAPPEN TO YOU

from the Paramount Picture AND THE ANGELS SING

Words by JOHNNY BURKE
Music by JAMES VAN HEUSEN

Don't count stars or you might stum - ble, _____

Some - one drops a sigh, and down you tum - ble.

Keep an eye on Spring, run when

church bells ring. It could hap - pen to

JAVA JIVE

Words and Music by MILTON DRAKE
and BEN OAKLAND

Lightly, with an easy beat

I love cof-fee, I love tea,___ I love the ja-va jive and it loves me.___

Cof-fee and tea___ and the jiv-in' and me,___ a cup, a cup, a cup, a cup, a cup!

I love ja-va, sweet and hot,___ Whoops! Mis-ter Mo-to, I'm a cof-fee pot.___

JERSEY BOUNCE

Words by ROBERT WRIGHT
Music by BOBBY PLATTER, TINY BRADSHAW,
ED JOHNSON and ROBERT WRIGHT

Easy Bounce

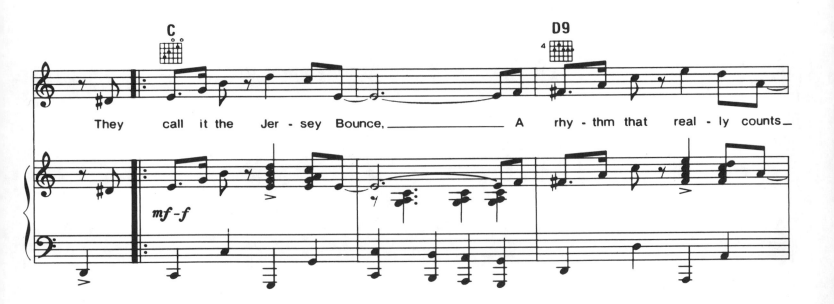

They call it the Jer-sey Bounce, _____ A rhy-thm that real-ly counts_

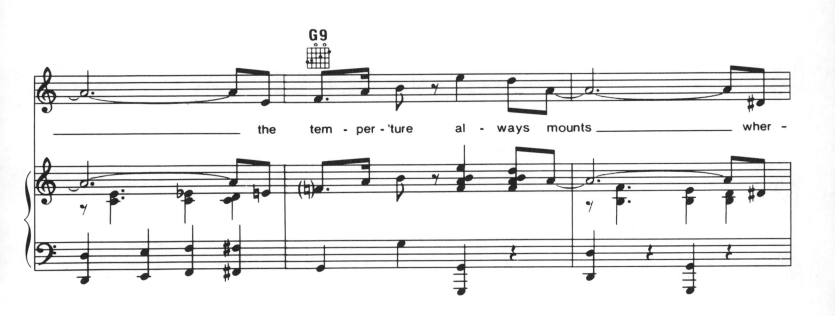

the tem-per-'ture al-ways mounts _____ wher-

JUKE BOX SATURDAY NIGHT

Words by AL STILLMAN
Music by PAUL McGRANE

Moderately

Mop-pin' up so-da pop rick-eys _____ to our heart's ___ de-light _____ danc-in' to swing-er-oo quick-ies, _____ juke box Sat-ur-day night. ___ Good-man and Ky-ser and Mil-

LAZY RIVER

Words and Music by HOAGY CARMICHAEL
and SIDNEY ARODIN

LEAN BABY

Lyric by ROY ALFRED
Music by BILLY MAY

THE MAN WITH THE HORN

Lyric by EDDIE DE LANGE
Music by JACK JENNEY, BONNIE LAKE
and EDDIE DE LANGE

LET'S DANCE

Words by FANNY BALDRIDGE
Music by GREGORY STONE and JOSEPH BONINE

MANHATTAN

Words by LORENZ HART
Music by RICHARD RODGERS

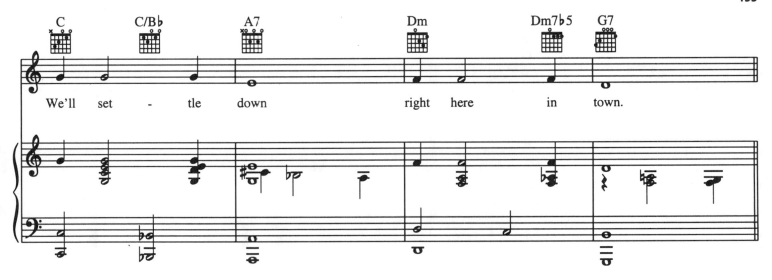

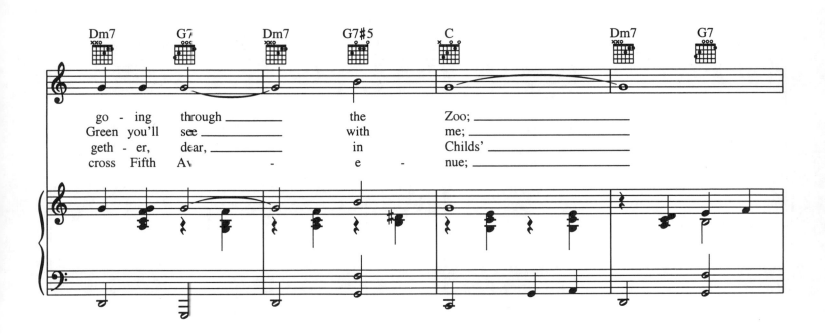

MEMORIES OF YOU

Lyric by ANDY RAZAF
Music by EUBIE BLAKE

MOOD INDIGO

Words and Music by DUKE ELLINGTON,
IRVING MILLS and ALBANY BIGARD

MOONGLOW

Words and Music by WILL HUDSON,
EDDIE DE LANGE and IRVING MILLS

Like some-one that has-n't an-y coun-try, _____ like a strang-er vis-it-ing from Mars, I went a-round a-lone, just like a roll-ing stone un-til I read a mes-sage in the stars:

MOONLIGHT IN VERMONT

Words and Music by JOHN BLACKBURN
and KARL SUESSDORF

(There Ought to Be A)
MOONLIGHT SAVING TIME

Words and Music by IRVING KAHAL
and HARRY RICHMAN

174

THE MUSIC GOES 'ROUND AND AROUND

Words by RED HODGSON
Music by EDWARD FARLEY and MICHAEL RILEY

MY SILENT LOVE

Words by EDWARD HEYMAN
Music by DANA SUESSE

OLD DEVIL MOON

Words by E.Y. HARBURG
Music by BURTON LANE

184

185

NEVERTHELESS
(I'm in Love with You)

Words and Music by BERT KALMAR
and HARRY RUBY

OPUS ONE

Words and Music by
SY OLIVER

Moderate Jump Tempo

I'm wrack-in' my brain, to think of a name, __ To give to this tune, so Per-ry can croon, __ And may-be Ol' Bing will give it a fling, __ And that'll start ev-'ry-one hum-min' the thing. __ The mel-o-dy's dumb, re-

PENTHOUSE SERENADE

Words and Music by WILL JASON
and VAL BURTON

Man - y swains have tried to make ro - man - tic, the cot - tage by the stream. Men of let - ters, po - ets quite pe - dan - tic, have used this played - out theme.

Ev - 'ry - thing will be quite cir - cum - spect, dear, on mod - ern lines ex - pressed. Love a - lone will be the ar - chi - tect dear, to build our lit - tle nest.

POLKA DOTS AND MOONBEAMS

Words by JOHNNY BURKE
Music by JIMMY VAN HEUSEN

SATURDAY NIGHT IS THE
LONELIEST NIGHT OF THE WEEK

Words by SAMMY CAHN
Music by JULE STYNE

SENTIMENTAL JOURNEY

Words and Music by BUD GREEN,
LES BROWN and BEN HOMER

Ev - 'ry roll-ing stone gets to feel a - lone when home, sweet home is far a - way. ____

I'm a roll-ing stone who's been so a - lone un - til to - day.

Gon - na take a sen - ti - men - tal jour-ney, gon - na set my

SMOKE RINGS

Words by NED WASHINGTON
Music by H. EUGENE GIFFORD

Where do they go _____ the
Where do they end _____ the

smoke rings I blow _ each night? _____
smoke rings I send _ on high? _____

SMALL FRY
from the Paramount Picture SING, YOU SINNERS

Words by FRANK LOESSER
Music by HOAGY CARMICHAEL

Here comes that good-for-noth-in' brat of a boy;___

he's such a dev-il I could whip him with joy.___

He's been ca-rous-in' at the bur-ley-cue.___

SNOWFALL

Lyrics by RUTH THORNHILL
Music by CLAUDE THORNHILL

SOLITUDE

Words and Music by DUKE ELLINGTON,
EDDIE DE LANGE and IRVING MILLS

SOUTH OF THE BORDER
(Down Mexico Way)

Words and Music by JIMMY KENNEDY
and MICHAEL CARR

can - dle - light she knelt to pray The mis - sion bells told me

That I must - n't stay South Of The Bor - der Down Mex - i - co

way Ay! Ay! Ay! Ay! Ay! Ay! Ay! Ay!

Ay! Ay! Ay! Ay! Ay! Ay! Ay! Ay!

rall. e dim.

8vb

STAR DUST

Words by MITCHELL PARISH
Music by HOAGY CARMICHAEL

we're a - part. You wan - dered down the lane and

far a - way, leav - ing me a song that will not

die. Love is now the star dust of yes - ter - day,

the mu - sic of the years gone by. Some - times I

STELLA BY STARLIGHT
from the Paramount Picture THE UNINVITED

Words by NED WASHINGTON
Music by VICTOR YOUNG

STEPPIN' OUT WITH MY BABY

from the Motion Picture Irving Berlin's EASTER PARADE

Words and Music by
IRVING BERLIN

STOMPIN' AT THE SAVOY

Words and Music by BENNY GOODMAN,
EDGAR SAMPSON, CHICK WEBB and ANDY RAZAF

SWEET SUE-JUST YOU

Words by WILL J. HARRIS
Music by VICTOR YOUNG

STORMY WEATHER
(Keeps Rainin' All the Time)

Lyric by TED KOEHLER
Music by HAROLD ARLEN

Don't know why _____ there's no sun up in the sky, storm-y weath-er, _____

since my {man}{gal} and I ____ ain't to-geth-er, _____ keeps rain-in' all ___ the time. _____

Life is bare, _____ gloom and mis-'ry ev-'ry-where, storm-y weath-er, _____

A STRING OF PEARLS

Words by EDDIE DE LANGE
Music by JERRY GRAY

Ba - by ___ here's ___ a five and dime, Ba - by ___ now's ___
Ba - by ___ { you ___ / I ___ } made quite a start, found the ___ way ___

___ a - bout the time for a ___ string ___ of pearls a - la
___ right to { my / your } heart with a ___ string ___ of pearls a - la

Wool - worth. ___
Wool - worth. ___
Ev - 'ry ___ pearl's ___ a star a - bove
Wait 'til ___ the ___ stars peek - a - boo,

'TAIN'T WHAT YOU DO
(It's the Way That Cha Do It)

Words and Music by SY OLIVER
and JAMES YOUNG

TAKE THE "A" TRAIN

Words and Music by
BILLY STRAYHORN

TANGERINE

from the Paramount Picture THE FLEET'S IN

Words by JOHNNY MERCER
Music by VICTOR SCHERTZINGER

South A-mer-i-can sto-ries ____ tell of a girl who's quite a dream, _ the beau-ty of her race. Though you doubt all the sto-ries ____ and think the tales are just a bit ex-

THAT OLD BLACK MAGIC

from the Paramount Picture STAR SPANGLED RHYTHM

Words by JOHNNY MERCER
Music by HAROLD ARLEN

That old black mag - ic has me in its ___ spell. ___ That old black mag - ic that you weave so ___ well. ___ Those

and down and down I go, 'round and 'round

I go like a leaf that's caught in the tide.

I should stay a - way but what can I do?

I hear your name and I'm a - flame,

THERE ARE SUCH THINGS

Words and Music by STANLEY ADAMS,
ABEL BAER and GEORGE W. MEYER

THERE! I'VE SAID IT AGAIN

By DAVE MANN
and REDD EVANS

THERE'LL BE SOME CHANGES MADE

Words by BILLY HIGGINS
Music by W. BENTON OVERSTREET

Additional Choruses

1. There's a change in your manner
   And a change in your way
   There was time once when you was O.K.
   You once said you saved ev'ry kiss for my sake
   Now you're giving all the girls an even break
   I'm gonna send out invitations to the men I know
   'Cause you're gettin' colder than an Eskimo
   I must have my lovin' or I'll fade away
   There'll be some changes made to-day
   There'll be some changes made.

2. For there's a change in your manner
   There's a change in your style
   And here of late you never wear a smile
   You don't seem to act like a real lover should
   You can't thrill your mamma if you're made of wood
   I gotta have a man who loves me like a real live Skeik
   With a tasty kiss that lingers for a week
   I'm not over sixty so it's time to say
   There'll be some changes made to-day
   There'll be some changes made.

3. For there's a change in your squeezin'
   There's a change in your kiss
   It used to have a kick that I now miss
   You'd set me on fire when you used to tease
   Now each time you call I just sit there and freeze
   You had a way of making love that made a hit with me
   One time you could thrill me but it's plain to see
   You're not so ambitious as you used to be
   There'll be some changes made by me
   There'll be some changes made.

4. There's a change in the weather
   There's a change in the sea
   From now on there'll be a change in me
   I'm tired of working all of my life
   I'm gonna grab a rich husband and be his wife
   I'm going to ride around in a big limousine
   Wear fancy clothes and put on plenty of steam
   No more tired puppies, will I treat you mean
   There'll be some changes made to-day
   There'll be some changes made.

5. For there's a change in your manner
   There's a change in your smile
   From now on you can't be worth my while
   I'm right here to tell you with you I'm thru
   Your brand of lovin' will never do
   I'm gettin' tired of eating just butter and bread
   I could enjoy a few pork chops instead
   You know variety is the spice of life they say
   There'll be some changes made to-day (I'll get mine)
   There'll be some changes made.

THE VERY THOUGHT OF YOU

Words and Music by
RAY NOBLE

I don't need your por - trait, dear, _____
I'm sue - ing your for dam - ag - es, _____

to call ___ you to mind, _____ For sleep - ing or
ex - cus - es won't do, _____ I'll on - ly be

wak - ing, dear, ___ I find; _____
sat - is - fied ___ with you; _____

The ver - y thought of you, _____ and I for -

THE THINGS WE DID LAST SUMMER

Words by SAMMY CAHN
Music by JULE STYNE

THIS YEAR'S KISSES

from the 20th Century Fox Motion Picture ON THE AVENUE

Words and Music by
IRVING BERLIN

TUXEDO JUNCTION

Words by BUDDY FEYNE
Music by ERSKINE HAWKINS,
WILLIAM JOHNSON and JULIAN DASH

WHAT'S NEW?

Words by JOHNNY BURKE
Music by BOB HAGGART

Bbm **C7#5** **C7** **Fm** **G7** **G7#5(b9)**

and you were sweet to of-fer your hand. __ I un-der-stand, __ a -

C6 **Eb9** **Eb7b9** **Ab** **Abmaj7** **Ab7**

dieu! Par-don my ask-ing what's new. _____

G7#5 **G7b5** **G7** **Cm** **Fm** **G7#5** **G7**

____ Of course you could-n't know, I have-n't changed, I

1 C **F** **C** **G7#5(b9)** **2 C** **F** **C**

still love you so. _____ What's new? __ still love you so. _____

WILLOW WEEP FOR ME

Words and Music by
ANN RONELL

YOU TURNED THE TABLES ON ME

Words by SIDNEY MITCHELL
Music by LOUIS ALTER

YOU'D BE SO NICE TO COME HOME TO

Words and Music by
COLE PORTER

It's not that you're fair-er, Than a lot of girls just as pleas-in', That I doff my hat as a wor-ship-per at your shrine,— It's